This book belongs to

....

....

Useful words

(in the order they appear in this book)

biscuits

crisps

fruit

grapes

hamburgers

jelly

lemonade

marshmallows

sandwiches

tea

Quarrelsome Queen's
Picnic

Ben's boat

Susan Welby

Quarrelsome Queen does not like to be kept waiting. So ...

Be quick, be quick,

Bouncy Ben.

But don't break the biscuits.

Come on, come on,

Clever Cat.

But don't crush the crisps.

Faster, faster,
Fireman Fred.
But mind the fruit
doesn't fall out.

Go, go,

Golden Girl.

You've got to get the

grapes there on time!

Hurry, hurry,

Hairy Hat Man.

But have you got

enough hamburgers?

Jump, jump,

Jumping Jim.

Just don't drop the jellies.

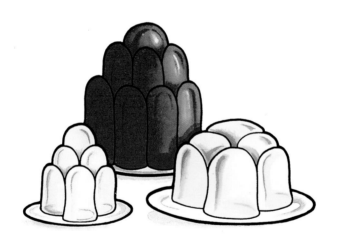

Don't be late,

Lamp Lady.

But don't leave without

the lemonade.

Move, move,

Munching Mike.

But mind the marshmallows.

Speed up, speed up,
Sammy Snake.
But don't let the
sandwiches slip.

Where's the tea,

Ticking Tess?

You're just in time for ...

... the Queen's picnic.

The Letterlanders

| Annie Apple | Bouncy Ben | Clever Cat | Dippy Duck | Eddy Elephant | Fireman Fred | Golden Girl |

| Hairy Hat Man | Impy Ink | Jumping Jim | Kicking King | Lucy Lamp Lady | Munching Mike |

| Naughty Nick | Oscar Orange | Poor Peter | Quarrelsome Queen | Robber Red | Sammy Snake | Ticking Tess |

| Uppy Umbrella | Vase of Violets | Wicked Water Witch | Max and Maxine | Yellow Yo-yo Man | Zig Zag Zebra |

Published by Collins Educational
An imprint of HarperCollins*Publishers* Ltd
77-85 Fulham Palace Road
London W6 8JB

First published 1998
Reprinted 1998, 2001

ISBN 0 00 303382 1

LETTERLAND® is a registered trademark of Lyn Wendon.

The author asserts the moral right to be identified as the author
of this work.

British Library Cataloguing in Publication Data
A catalogue record for this book is available from the British Library.

Written by Susan Welby
Illustrated by Jan West
Colouring by Dulcie Tobin
Designed by Michael Sturley and Sally Boothroyd
Consultant: Lyn Wendon, originator of Letterland

Printed by Printing Express, Hong Kong

Letterland ®

Letterland At Home is a range of books, cassettes and flashcards that uses a fun approach to help children to read and write. Three colour-coded Stages will help you to choose the books that are right for your child.

Stage 1

Available from all good bookshops.

For an information leaflet about Letterland call 0181 307 4052.

Stage 2

Stage 3

For younger children, a colourful range of first skills activity books has been developed.